Wanda L. Scott

LIFE and LOVE

For Life & Love You Have To Know What You Are In Agreement With!

The Identity for Life Teaching Series

Book I

Wanda L. Scott
Forward by Rev. Dr. Lee P. Washington

LIFE and LOVE
For Life & Love You Have To Know What You Are In Agreement With!

Copyright © 2015 Wanda L. Scott
Originally portions of this book were copyrighted in ©2006 as *Identity Theft*: *Strengthening Our Youth Through the Grey Areas of Life*

All rights reserved. No part of this book may be reproduced or transmitted in any form or by any means, electronic or mechanical, including photocopying, recording or by any information storage and retrieval system, without written permission from the author, except for the inclusion of brief quotations in a review.

Unless otherwise noted, Scripture quotations are from the New King James Version of the Bible.
Scripture quotations noted by NKJV are taken from the Holy Bible, New King James Version copyright © 1979, 1980, 1982 by Thomas Nelson, Inc.
Scripture quotations noted by RSV are taken from the Revised Standard Version of the Bible, copyright © 1946, 1952, and 1971 by the National Council of the Churches of Christ in the USA. Used by permission. All rights reserved.

Editor: Wanda J. S. Banks
Cover Design by Preston Spencer
Inside Layout and Design by Wanda L. Scott

ISBN 978-0-9761322-5-7 Paperback
ISBN 978-0-9761322-8-8   eBook

10 9 8 7 6 5 4 3 2 1

Published through the Image Institute
(A Division of WLS Enterprises)
www.Image-Institute.org

Printed in the Unites States of America

Wanda L. Scott

For Workshops, Teaching or Speaking Engagements for this book you can view the current scheduled dates for the Image Institute and request bookings at www.WandaLScott.com.

Life & Love

ACKNOWLEDGEMENTS

As I prepare to release this book (the first of two) of what was originally the book **Identity Theft**: *Strengthening Our Youth Through the Grey Areas of Life*, there are so many people that come to mind who were of so much support to me back in 2007. I first want to thank my then Pastor, Rev. Dr. Lee P. Washington for being a true man of God, and always supporting my writing dreams. His review encouraged me and solidified the journey of this book going to print. I thank Rev. Carey James, who wrote the original Introduction to this book. He and his wife are beautiful people and I pray God is continuing to bless them in his ministry and in their family. I want to mention Donte and Kim at Lazarus Graphics who for the original book brought my cover to life. Additionally to everyone who took the time to review the book, I cannot name them all but your feedback was invaluable.

As always I am thankful to God and the power of the Holy Spirit that empowers me to write and share God's Word in this form.

These books have really been a journey looking back at my life's path until now. What does it mean to accept the Lord at 7 years old, and how does a child process that pull from God to accept Jesus. What were my next steps, influences, and how was Christ-likeness modeled before me? These questions led me to seek out God's Word and how He wants these questions answered in order to live a life pleasing to God day by day & to raise children in His image and likeness. I am so blessed that the Lord has kept me and allowed me to make it through the wrong choices in the grey areas, and by His mercy live to try and make the right choices in the grey areas. We all have a path to take, lessons to be learned, and opportunities to see God in it each and every time. I hope that this book will help those coming behind me and those on their present journey to keep their eyes focused on not only God's mercy, love and grace, but also on God's will for each of our lives. It is only in seeing, fearing, loving and yielding to Christ that we will truly learn our own identity, thus being a part of the kingdom of God helping His will to be done and His kingdom to come here on earth as it is in heaven.

Thank you God for your Holy Spirit and the gifting and anointing you have placed on my life. May the grace of the Lord Jesus Christ, and the love of God, and the communion of the Holy Spirit *be* with you all. Amen.

Working Every Day to Walk in His Will,
Wanda L. Scott

TABLE OF CONTENTS

FORWARD 8

INTRODUCTION 9

WHO ARE YOU? 10

YOU: DESIGNED BY GOD 24

WHAT IS REAL LOVE 34

AN AUTHENTIC RELATIONSHIP ... 45

GOD'S FAMILY PORTRAIT 58

Bibliography 72

Scripture References 73

FORWARD

I was in conversation recently with a group of Pastors and the subject of gender identification became the topic of discussion. One of my Pastor friends passionately expressed her concerns over the struggles our Youth are having in this area and the impact it is having in the schools.

We pondered over the issue, prayed and sought to develop a pragmatic approach that would empower our Youth who are wrestling with this "grey area" of their lives. Characteristically, as pastors we do not look to one another to compete or criticize one another, we simply talk out our concerns, feelings, or thoughts and through prayer work out solutions.

I think this book is wonderful in how Wanda Scott provides substance for those that are facing grey areas. *Life and Love* is a thought provoking book that demonstrates how the Holy Spirit grows in us and forms Christ in our lives.

We are in a fight for truth and God-reality. Mental habits are formed by people training us to get what we think we have coming to us as a child. We desperately need books like this that challenge us to discipline our minds to think God, who God is, and what God is doing in and among us.

Rev. Dr. Lee P. Washington
Senior Pastor, Reid Temple AME Church

INTRODUCTION

The ***Identity for Life*** teaching series of books lays out for us the scripture that feeds us the fundamentals of our God-identity. Each book shows us how the Word of God applies to our everyday living, walking in love toward God and others. There is a specific focus on personal accountability by agreeing with God's Word, and our responsibility to those we come in contact with every day.

Each book deals with different aspects of our identity in Christ, and each one builds on the other with scripture and further biblical insight. As we form our identity in Jesus Christ, choices are made in what this series calls the "grey areas" of our lives. As we take a look at life, there are many different directions or paths that can be taken spiritually. Depending on which path you take, or which choice you make, you could be set in a direction that eventually leads you towards God's will for your life, wondering in the grey area or destruction. On the path of life are these grey areas which can be filled with people, opportunities, obstacles, circumstances, and choices. It is in this grey area that one can find God and change his/her final destination. It is in this grey area that one can make choices that help them find "purpose", "peace", "prosperity", and "abundant life" in Christ Jesus.

These Identity Principles can help you profess and confess who and what you are in Christ Jesus. When we understanding our identity and agree with God, it brings Life and Love.

1
WHO ARE YOU?

Philippians 2 ^{14} *Do all things without grumbling or questioning,* ^{15} *that you may be blameless and innocent, children of God without blemish in the midst of a crooked and perverse generation, among whom you shine as lights in the world,* ^{16} *holding fast the word of life………..(NRSV)*

WE ALL HAVE A UNIQUE IDENTITY. We are each fashioned differently, sometimes in drastic ways, sometimes in subtle ways. We each have a different fingerprint, retina print, and DNA. Our family, the place we grow up in, and the culture of the people around us, all intermingle to form our personality and character. Many different things in this world influence our lives and who we become. Ultimately the choices we make, and the person we become depends on the choices we make as an individual; no one can make these choices for us. When each of us makes these choices on our own, we take ownership of our lives. Only then do we make sure that we don't get lost in this world.

Identity – Psychological vs. Spiritual
Let's take a step back further. There is a Creator of each and every individually unique person. He is God; the Alpha and the Omega, the Beginning and the End. His mastery is how we have these unique characteristics. God does not just design our exterior uniqueness, but He fashions our lives to make our intrinsic character, which defines our very soul and spirit. He uses everything from our parents to our prom date to guide us to be the person He desires for us to be. In this predestined journey we still have to make the right choices to live up to our God given potential; God gives us a choice called 'free will'. In

Romans Chapter 6, the Word of God explains to us that whoever you choose to obey, you are a slave to. So the ultimate choice is to look to God and His word, and not the world for guidance.

> What then? Shall we sin because we are not under law but under grace? Certainly not! Do you not know that to whom you present yourselves slaves to obey, you are that one's slaves whom you obey, **whether of sin leading to death, or of obedience leading to righteousness**?
>
> For when you were slaves of sin, you were free in regard to righteousness. **What fruit did you have then in the things of which you are now ashamed?** For the end of those things is death. But now having been set free from sin, and having become slaves of God, you have your fruit to holiness, and the end, everlasting life. For the wages of sin is death, but the gift of God is eternal life in Christ Jesus our Lord (Romans 6:15-16; 20-23).

Identity Principle

God does not just design our exterior uniqueness, but He fashions our lives to make our intrinsic character, which defines our soul and spirit.

Moments of decision come to each of us at different times, as God calls us to be His Son's disciple. When God calls us, He wants us to get to know Him and learn to live according to the Word of God. We either obey God by accepting His call and begin growing closer to Jesus, or we are disobedient and continue on in our own destructive path doing things the way we want to do them – how we have always done them. In learning about and loving Jesus we find out what true life is and looks like. The more we ignore God, the more we look for other things and other people to follow and cling to. When we look to that other person or thing we begin to take on characteristics similar to it. We are identified with that object, and it can pull us further away from the guidance of God, our Creator. If we don't choose the Lord Jesus, we seem to constantly search for something to fill the space where God should be in our lives. Our spirit will always be void of the fulfillment that only God's love and comfort can bring. Alan Jones in *Exploring Spiritual Direction* states, "We believe that there is One whose service is perfect freedom. Thus, for a Christian the answer is clear: Christians are those who have surrendered to God in Christ and the Spirit calls us into companionship with one another. It is all a question of surrender, of self-abandonment, and we need the fellowship of our fellow pilgrims to do this in a creative way. We cannot help but tremble on the brink of surrender, but it is our companions who give us the courage to jump."[1] We must surrender to God's call so that we can find that perfect love to guide us in this life.

Identity Principle

When we identify with another person or thing we begin to take on characteristics similar to it.

As a young person reaches an age where they begin to understand the need to try and figure out things for themselves; they base these decisions on what they have been introduced to or influenced by in their lives. It is here that they start on a path to destruction or to enlightenment; it is here that they start to find their own way or they are blessed enough to start seeking God's way. Is it really that black and white you ask? Well no, but the destination of the path we go down is. It is on the path that you find the grey area. This grey area is filled with people, opportunities, obstacles, circumstances, and choices. ***It is in this grey area that one can find God and change his/her final destination. It is in this grey area that one can make choices that help them find "purpose", "peace", "prosperity", and "abundant life" in Jesus Christ.***

Self-Worth

What do the young people you interact with or your own children think about themselves? Do they think they think they should dress like they are in 'rap video' or act like they are in a 'Housewives of' show, or do they care more about being an intelligent, loving individual? Do they feel like they are not worth anyone's attention or loving touch, because you never take the time to ask them about their day or issues they might be having? Are they searching for love in the streets because you don't show them any love at home? Do they know that love is not sex, and that love does not take, it gives?

The world will take every opportunity to tell our children who they should be, and what they should be doing. All are acceptable, from the images they see on TV and magazine ads, to what they see other so called role models doing. It is our responsibility to let them know their value and self-worth. They need to know that they were fearfully and wonderfully made (Psalm 139:4). They should understand that they are unique, and have an option to pray to their Creator for strength and wisdom. Our children need positive re-enforcement from us on their abilities and option to be different from others around them in this world. We must encourage them to believe in themselves, and believe that we love them and will be there for them. If we don't someone or something in the street will convince them that they are their only option of support and guidance. Our children need to be loved and nurtured so they will know their worth.

Our Self-Worth

Do we as the parent, care giver or nurturer know our self-worth in order to pass it along to our children? Can we push through our own negative cycles, pain from broken homes, and abuse, to properly instill this self-worth into the young people of today? Only with God and the power of His Holy Spirit can we give our children what we never had. What do you think about yourself? Charles Stanley in his book, *Success God's Way,* reveals that "how you think or feel about yourself is going to be projected in the way you behave."² Only God can pick us up and turn us around to be the godly parents and care givers we need to be. He is the only one who can help us and our children understand our self-worth.

Accountability

What kind of example are we to our children? When they are faced with decisions and influenced by things outside of the home, will they make a choice to be different because we have shown them that different is ok? When asked to try alcohol, even though we told them not to drink before a certain age, will they still say "why not" because we have not explained its harmful effects and consequences on young people's lives? When another young person is smoking, will they think it is cool? Or will they say it is not healthy, because neither one of their parents smoke, and has also talked to them about the harm it could do to their body and mind, causing addiction.

Identity Principle

We must live a life pleasing to God, so that our children will know what that type of godly life looks like.

Do we live by the age old adage "do as I say and not as I do", or do we walk what we talk? Our children will eventually act out what they see and hear in the home. We must step up to the plate and be accountable for our actions even if we are not doing it for ourselves but for the young people we are influencing today. If we don't who will? If we don't, what will become of them faced with the examples they are given in this world? If we don't hold ourselves accountable today, we will be held accountable on judgment day. We must live a life pleasing to God, so that our children will know what that type of godly life looks like.

"How you think about a child results in the way you speak to that child, what you give to that child, and how you treat that child."[3] What message are you sending your child? Are you building up their self-worth? So many of the parents today have children at a very young age and don't fully have time to live, mature, and grow in God. The demand of parenting can lead to feelings of resentment and anger. We should ask ourselves "What kinds of thoughts am I planting in my child's mind about himself, and about me as a parent, and about our family?"[4]

> "Do as I say and not as I do!"

What do we have to do to be accountable to our families in the passing on of the Word of God? God laid out a plan to Moses to give to His chosen people the Israelites - as we are His chosen people now - on how they could stay true and accountable to Him and receive His blessings.

> Therefore you shall lay up these words of mine in your heart and in your soul, and bind them as a sign on your hand, and they shall be as frontlets between your eyes. You shall teach them to your children, speaking of them when you sit in your house, when you walk by the way, when you lie down, and when you rise up. And you shall write them on the doorposts of your house and on your gates, that your days and the days of your children may be multiplied in the land of which the LORD swore to your fathers to give them, like the days of the heavens above the earth. (Deuteronomy 11:18-21)

The Word of God is true today, yesterday, and tomorrow. It is living, and we can always stand on God's Word to find truth and direction. By following these passages above we show that we know and understand how important the truth of God's Word is. When we do these things we know that we are being accountable before God.

Influences

Who or what has influenced your life? What examples have you chosen to follow? The answer to these questions steer us on our journey through the grey areas of our lives. Think back on your life and the decisions you have made. What influenced that decision? Was it fear, did you learn from someone else's mistake, or were you pressured into it because someone believed in themselves more than you believed in yourself to make your own decision? We must encourage our children to "Never count yourself out. As long as you are alive and the Lord is resident in you, you are very much "in the game"".[5]

The world as an influence is a different place than it was 30 years ago. There is very little respect for life, morality, or the elder generation. There is a lack of accountability that used to be in society; this opens the door for individuals to place blame on others, and makes them think that they can do whatever they feel. This adds additional pressure on our young people. The different influences that they have to deal with force them to come to a place of decision in the grey area. These days the decisions that are faced in the grey area for our young people lend more toward evil influences than positive godly influences. A lot of young people never see or hear about God in their early years. Life is so hard that all they hear about from their parents or family is school and money problems. There is very little room for God, love, or peace.

> **Young people can make choices based on ignorance, morality, peer pressure, or force.**

The church or body of Christ as an influence is different these days also. In a lot of families today examples of those who follow God or have a relationship with the Lord Jesus are absent. So the Lord's witness has become silent in these families. This has deterred our ability to be a witness for the gospel to all nations, nonetheless in our families. We need to show the love and care of God past our sanctuary doors into our places of work, our schools, and to people we see day by day. This silence turns into the lack of giving to those who need Jesus' message and has assisted the world in its overwhelming influence. The world is willing to protest and march in the streets to disband everything that God has placed of Himself in it. The body of Christ, as individuals appear to just sit and shake their heads while preachers preach about what should be going on, all the while laws are passed, articles are written, and constitutional amendments are overturned. We need to "be the light" in our own homes, neighborhoods and jobs in order to break the silence and be the servants and witnesses God has called us to be. Young people don't see us doing the work of God. Young people see action and excitement in the world on a consistent basis, while they only see action and "good feelings" in the church on Sunday. They need to see the love of God in action through us helping others and giving of ourselves.

Identity Principle

Our children need to see the love of God in action through us helping others and giving of ourselves.

Choices

Young people can make choices based on ignorance, morality, peer pressure, or force. When forced to make a choice we must equip our young people to make informed, moral and definitive decisions. They must be empowered with the Truth and see examples of adults making *right* decisions. Just as we as adults do not like to make certain decisions, our children feel pressure in these situations also; so we must give them a foundation that speaks to them immediately of the right choice to make. If we do not arm them with the information to make these right choices, then they will rely on others or their own learned ideas from the world to form an opinion. This is dangerous but avoidable, if we just do what is right regardless of how busy our lives have us. Some busyness is just a distraction so that we don't give the Lord the time He requires to give us guidance. We must take the time to make a difference in the lives of our children and give them a choice we might not have had at their age. As we empower our young people with the truth of God's Word, this will help them get to know who God is and how He interacts with His people as we read the bible with them, encouraging them to read the bible themselves and be accountable in the "ways of God" in front of them. The life we live serving God and others empowers our children to see a different way to live. This will help them conquer a pattern of ignorant choices, and empower them to make morally sound choices. God's Word provides a moral standard, and gives them knowledge of what is truth and what are the lies of Satan.

Identity Principle

If we know our identity, we know we find it in the Word of God.

When we develop a sense of self-worth in our children, they are less likely to succumb to peer pressure. When we help them identify who they can be in God, and the power He would provide them, they are less likely to be forced into things. God's Word teaches them how to keep themselves out of certain situations that could be harmful to them. God will help them make right decisions and armor them with a choice.

The World

> Do not love the world or the things in the world. If anyone loves the world, the love of the Father is not in him. For all that is in the world—the lust of the flesh, the lust of the eyes, and the pride of life—is not of the Father but is of the world. And the world is passing away, and the lust of it; but he who does the will of God abides forever. (1 John 2:15-17 NKJV)

If we know our identity, we know we find it in the Word of God. The Word is our source for all aspects of our lives, because the Word is our key to God. So we live by the Word, but we live in the world. The world represents those that do not recognize that there is a God. The world represents those who make no effort to live by or reverence God in His Word. The world also represents the devil and his legion of evil spirits that inhabit the world and use people who are unaware or let him.

> And the great dragon was cast out, that old serpent, called the Devil, and Satan, which deceiveth the whole world: he was cast out into the earth, and his angels were cast out with him. And I heard a loud voice saying in heaven, Now is come salvation, and strength, and the kingdom of our God, and the power of his Christ: for the accuser of our brethren is cast down, which accused them before our God day and night. And they overcame him by the blood of the Lamb, and by the word of their testimony; and they loved not their lives unto the death. Therefore rejoice, ye heavens, and ye that dwell in them. Woe to the inhabiters of the earth and of the sea! for the devil is come down unto you, having great wrath, because he knoweth that he hath but a short time.(Revelation 12:9-12)

It is clear what the intentions of the devil are here on this earth. He is the prince of the power of the air, a spirit who works in those who are disobedient to God (Ephesians 2:2). Satan will work as the deceiver and the accuser to steal, kill, and destroy life if we let him (John 10:10). We must choose life with Jesus in the Word, and not the world's ways which lead to destruction.

And you He made alive, who were dead in trespasses and sins, in which you once walked according to the course of this world, according to the prince of the power of the air, the spirit who now works in the sons of disobedience, among whom also we all once conducted ourselves in the lusts of our flesh, fulfilling the desires of the flesh and of the mind, and were by nature children of wrath, just as the others (Ephesians 2:1-3 NKJV).

The Grey Area

"Never use your race, your color, your lack of education, or your background as an excuse. God knows all about your race and color and culture – He caused you to be born with that race, color and into that culture. What you don't know, God knows. What you don't have, God has."[6] In the grey area we have to make our choices and decisions based on knowledge of our true identity. We have to have had other wise adults to have spoken into our lives so that we can dare to be different.

> But you *are* a chosen generation, a royal priesthood, a holy nation, His own special people, that you may proclaim the praises of Him who called you out of darkness into His marvelous light (1 Peter 2:9 NKJV)

AGREEMENT

DECLARATION: *Repeat these out loud...and then answer the question.*

1. ***I agree that I am one-of-a-kind created by God uniquely.*** Name one thing about you that is unique.

2. ***I agree that I am fearfully and wonderfully made, because whatever God creates is marvelous!***
Name one way you are wonderful.

3. ***I agree with God's definition of the world, and I will not love the things of the world, instead I will trust the Word of God!***
Would any of your actions fit with those in the world?

Action for Abundant Life

AWARENESS: Do you believe that your actions affect those around you and your witness for Christ? Can you give an example of when this has happened in your life?

AWARENESS: How have you been unprepared to make choices in your life? Would knowing what you know now in the Word of God have changed your choice?

UNDERSTANDING: Which Identity Principle in this chapter did you relate to the most? Why?

Wanda L. Scott

Who is wise?
Who will care?
To share the truth of God's love to children everywhere?

What choices will we make?
What example will we set?
Let us look to God,
the truth of His Word we will never regret.

WLS

2
YOU: DESIGNED BY GOD

***Genesis 1**[27] So God created man in his own image, in the image of God he created him; male and female he created them. [28] And God blessed them, and God said to them, "Be fruitful and multiply, and fill the earth and subdue it; and have dominion over the fish of the sea and over the birds of the air and over every living thing that moves upon the earth." (NRSV)*

WE ARE ALL CREATED BY GOD. He is the creator and ruler of all the heavens and earth (see Genesis 1). Yet in our schools, in most common literature and popular writings, our children are taught the Theory of Evolution stating that they evolved from monkeys, the Big Bang Theory, or Intelligent Design. This is what they learn in school and in the streets, where do they learn the truth about God?

It is your responsibility, if you are a child of God, to teach your children in the home, and have them participate in life with other believers (body of Christ). This is a great responsibility since we are all born in sin, and must acknowledge and accept Jesus Christ as our Lord and Savior for ourselves. Once this happens we are not just created by God, we are children of God. Let's look at some scriptures that explain the *identity* of a child of God:

> Every one who believes that Jesus is the Christ is a child of God, and every one who loves the parent loves the child. (1 John 5:1 NRSV)

> But to all who received him, who believed in his name, he gave power to become children of God (John 1:12 NRSV)

> See what love the Father has given us that we should be called children of God; and so we are. The reason why the world does not know us is that it did not know him. (1 John 3:1 NRSV)

Identity Principle

To be a child of God we are accepting Jesus Christ as our Lord and Savior.

To be a child of God we are accepting Jesus Christ as our Lord and Savior. This acknowledgement distinguishes us from all other religions who call on the name of God. This acceptance states that we believe that Jesus is the Son of God; and that He died on the cross and rose again to save us from our sins, so that we might repent and be born again. God shines His light into our heart so that we can understand and are open to the revelation of the knowledge of Jesus Christ (2 Corinth. 4:6). From then on we are called to be disciples of Jesus, and to follow God by obeying His will and His way. This is an awesome task that requires just as much of us as it cost God his only begotten Son.

> It is the Spirit himself bearing witness with our spirit that we are children of God (Romans 8:16)

> This means that it is not the children of the flesh who are the children of God, but the children of the promise are reckoned as descendants. (Romans 9:8)

When we accept Jesus, we receive His Spirit to lead and guide us as we grow in God's Word. The Holy Spirit lives in each of us as a gift to empower us to live according to God's Word. We must from then on study the Word of God, and listen to the Holy Spirit to learn how to walk in the spirit and not in the flesh. We study the Word of God by reading the bible, and other activities like bible study and prayer alone and with other believers (children of God). We listen to the Holy Spirit as we read the Word of God and pray to God, asking Him to help us learn His voice and the promptings of the Holy Spirit guiding us along the way. This is only possible because we were born again of spirit, not of flesh, but by faith in Jesus Christ. Our professed faith in Jesus Christ helps us to start living a spiritual life that is different from the physical or flesh-filled life we used to. We must allow God's Spirit to help us die to the world and our old ways, and let our new life emerge as we grow in the Spirit of the Lord (2 Corinthians 5:17). When we become new by the Spirit of God, we must actively make an effort to change our ways and take on the way of Jesus Christ left to us in the bible. We renew our minds by the Holy Spirit, given by Jesus to help us grow in His Word for this new life. We are then spiritually the seed of Abraham through the promise of the coming of the Lord Jesus Christ to reconcile us all to God as we saw earlier in Romans chapter 9, verse 8.

> In this the children of God and the children of the devil are manifest: Whoever does not practice righteousness is not of God, nor *is* he who does not love his brother. (1 John 3:10 NKJV)

> By this we know that we love the children of God, when we love God and obey his commandments. (1 John 5:2 NRSV)

Identity Principle

Walking in the Spirit is living according to the "teachings of the bible" by the power of the Holy Spirit.

Walking in the Spirit is living according to the "teachings of God" by the power of His Holy Spirit. We should show the evidence of God's deliverance and grace in our lives. We are graced with love in our hearts that manifests as we become closer to our Savior. This love, along with the Word of God convicts us to do right and love others as we would love ourselves. The Holy Spirit assists us in our walk with God by leading, guiding, and directing us in the path that we should go. As we make a constructive effort to obey, the better we are able to tune into the Spirit's attempts to communicate with us.

Losing Our Identity to Christ

> I have been crucified with Christ; it is no longer I who live, but Christ lives in me; and the life which I now live in the flesh I live by faith in the Son of God, who loved me and gave Himself for me. (Galatians 2:20 NKJV)

In taking on and understanding our true identity in Christ, one of the hardest concepts to comprehend and internalize in our everyday lives is the fact that we are not to live according to our own will. The problem is that we have been granted "free will", as the Lord will not force Himself on us. He says that He stands at the door and knocks (Rev. 3:20), and it is our responsibility to accept Him into our lives. Once we accept Him we have the gift of salvation, and we must no longer live in the flesh, but in the Spirit of Christ Jesus. The only way to do this is to walk in the Spirit by beginning to know and understand God's will for our everyday lives.

> But the manifestation of the Spirit is given to each one for the profit of all (1 Corinthians 12:7 NKJV)

> Examine yourselves as to whether you are in the faith. Test yourselves. Do you not know yourselves, that Jesus Christ is in you?—unless indeed you are disqualified. But I trust that you will know that we are not disqualified. (2 Corinthians 13:5-6 NKJV)

In examining and testing ourselves we stay in touch with the Spirit of Truth that dwells inside us, and brings us to the knowledge of God through Christ. By examining our behavior we can see if we are qualified, and able to uplift and encourage the body of Christ to grow so that we all will profit in living out what God wants for His people here on earth. We are able to examine our character to see if the true identity of Christ is in us.

In a world of "I" and "Me", the Word of God reminds us that we are one body in Christ, and that we cannot function without one another. We see in verse 5 above how Paul is inspired to encourage the church body at Corinth to "examine" and "test" themselves in their faith in Christ. Have you looked at yourself through the eyes of God lately? When is the last time you read the Word of God and examined where you lined up to what God wills for your life?

Identity Principle

We are not to live according to our own will obeying our flesh

Have you empowered yourself with the Word of God so that it can work in you? Or do you still walk as if you are powerless to the world? Jesus Christ is in you, and in His Word it says that we should be of good cheer, because He has overcome the world (John 16:33). The gift of salvation is the indwelling presence of the Holy Spirit. Does your spirit acknowledge and live by promptings of the Holy Spirit so you can know the truth of the Word of God for yourself?

As we grow by reading the Word of God and hearing the Word of God, we are transformed day by day to remove our will and say 'Lord your will be done'. In this effort we give up what we want for our lives and only live through Christ Jesus who lives in us (by His Word and Spirit). The Lord loves us and has given each of us a measure of faith to grow to become who He has called us to be as we take on His true character of love.

Certainty in Our Identity

> Therefore He is also able to save to the uttermost those who come to God through Him, since He always lives to make intercession for them. (Hebrews 7:25 NKJV)

Since we know our true identity is in Christ, we must examine ourselves to see if we are truly living for Christ. Are we walking in the Spirit of God displaying the character of Jesus Christ? Have you noticed behavior that unnerves you to the point where you wonder because you do "certain things" are you really saved? Do you ever question your salvation? Well, we must not forget that it is not us or anything within our own power that can save us. Salvation is a gift (Ephesians 2:8-10), and we must learn how to seek God and let Him do the work in us. Only in this way can we overcome the carnal nature that we display as children of God.

> For by grace you have been saved through faith, and that not of yourselves; it is the gift of God, not of works, lest anyone should boast. For we are His workmanship, created in Christ Jesus for good works, which God prepared beforehand that we should walk in them (Ephesians 2:8-10 NKJV).

We see in this passage of Hebrews chapter 7 that the only person who can completely save us is Jesus Christ. Verse 25 states that …because Jesus Christ lives forever…, He is the only one who can completely save through continuous intercession. What does that tell you? It tells me that we will be messing up in one area or another until Jesus comes back for us. No one is perfect but God. As we allow His Holy Spirit to change us, we are in a state of perfecting different areas of our lives. This does not mean that we cannot walk holy and righteous in His sight, it just means that there will always be another area of improvement that God shows us about ourselves to rely on Him to help us fix. As we obey we are perfected in God's eyes in that moment of obedience. Only when we live our lives following God's Spirit through Christ (Colossians 3:3) can we do "good". Even Jesus asked the rich man why does he call Him good, because there is only One that is good, and that is God (Luke 18:18).

> For you died, and your life is hidden with Christ in God (Colossians 3:3 NKJV)

We should be comforted in the fact that through faith in Jesus Christ we are saved, not by anything we can do. We can receive God's peace as long as we are repentant and moving in God's will for our lives. We have Jesus always living to intercede for us, perfecting His identity in and through us.

The Grey Area

Knowing our true identity in God we are able to make key choices when we enter into the grey areas of our lives. If at a young age we start to recognize who we are and what our place is in this world, we make better decisions. These decisions we make become harder and harder as we grow older, and have a larger impact on our lives. This initial knowledge of self gives us a fighting chance during our navigation down life's path. If we start with the faith that we can be a child of God we are moving toward life. If we don't even know that we are created by God and can be His child we are moving toward death. Let's work so that more of our young people know their true identity as a creation of God, and their potential to be a child of God. Dr. Myles Monroe concludes in his book, *Understanding The Purpose and Power of Men,* that "The question of identity is a global problem. I have traveled to many nations, and I have concluded that most of the world is suffering from what I call the "consequences of ignorance of purpose". In every nation, in every community, no matter what language the citizens speak or what color their skin is, people are experiencing a common dilemma. They are suffering the debilitating effects of a misconception of purpose. They don't understand who they really are and therefore aren't living up to their full potential in life."[1]

Identity Principle

We are saved through faith in Jesus Christ, not by anything we can do.

AGREEMENT

DECLARATION: *Repeat these out loud...and then answer the question.*

1. ***I agree that I am a child of God because of my faith that Jesus is the Son of God.*** Can you remember the day you accepted Christ as your Savior?

2. ***I agree that the Holy Spirit lives inside of me and is a gift from God!*** Name one way you recognize the presence of the Holy Spirit in your life.

3. ***I agree NOT to live according to my own will. I am empowered by the Holy Spirit to obey God's will!***

4. ***I agree that I am saved through faith in Jesus Christ, not by anything I can do.*** Have you ever tried to earn salvation?

Action for Abundant Life

AWARENESS: Do you know who you are in Christ? How does this affect your day-to-day actions?

AWARENESS: Have you shared with your children or young family members the truth about the God who created them for a purpose?

UNDERSTANDING: Which Identity Principle in this chapter did you relate to the most?   Why?

Who Am I?
You are a king,
destined for a prosperous life
bearing fruit, doing wondrous things.

Who Am I?
You are a queen,
influencing a generation
glowing in the light of Jesus,
to Him all the glory you bring.

How do you know this?
Jesus came for us all.
To seek and save those who are lost.
We just have to answer His call.

Embrace your identity in Christ Jesus,
His Holy Spirit will empower you
and will forever more be with you.

WLS

3
WHAT IS REAL LOVE

1 Corinthians 13^7 Love bears all things, believes all things, hopes all things, endures all things. (NRSV)

THE LORD LOVES US SO MUCH MORE than we can comprehend with our limited human minds. That is why when we are called to acknowledge the Lord God shines His light into our hearts so that we can have the knowledge of Him and His love. We cannot intellectualize why this omnipotent Being would love us so, especially knowing our faults and inconsistencies.

> For God, who commanded the light to shine out of darkness, hath shined in our hearts, to give the light of the knowledge of the glory of God in the face of Jesus Christ. (2 Corinthians 4:6)

The Lord's definition of love is innocent and pure, unassuming and incorruptible. We must truly seek His wisdom, and have a desire for the "teachings of God" to display His love for ourselves and those around us.

We must have a clear understanding of who we are in God, and who He is to us. Our personal relationship with Him is the foundation for truth, understanding, and love everlasting. Through Him and the guidance of the Holy Spirit we can manifest the fruit of the Spirit, love...real love. The world's definition of love pales in comparison to real love, or agape love as defined by God. The world's love is based on emotions and adheres to the oneness of lust. According to The American Heritage Dictionary three of the definitions of love are: *A deep, tender, ineffable feeling of affection and solicitude toward a person, such as that arising from kinship, recognition of attractive qualities, or a sense of underlying oneness; A feeling of intense desire and attraction toward a person with whom one is disposed to make a pair; the emotion of sex and romance; Sexual passion; Sexual intercourse; A love affair.* If we take the time to read the entire chapter of 1 Corinthians 13, we can see a striking difference between love as defined by the world and the love of Jesus Christ.

> Love suffers long *and* is kind; love does not envy; love does not parade itself, is not puffed up; does not behave rudely, does not seek its own, is not provoked, thinks no evil; does not rejoice in iniquity, but rejoices in the truth; bears all things, believes all things, hopes all things, endures all things. Love never fails.. (1 Corinthians 13:4-8 NKJV).

This difference is what we as humans and children of God struggle with every day to live up to. The first and greatest commandment is to love God with all our heart, mind and soul, and to love our neighbors as ourselves. Only God can help us love ourselves and others that way.

Identity Principle

We are commanded to love and we are responsible to pass this love on to our children as we are compelled by the overwhelming love of God toward us

---

It is imperative that we walk in the love that God has shown us. We are commanded to love, we are responsible to pass this love on to our children, and we are compelled in all of this by the overwhelming love that we feel when we become intimately familiar with our Lord and Savior Jesus Christ. By this shall all men know that ye are my disciples, if ye have love one to another (John 13:35). If we are truly to be distinguished as disciples of Christ by our love, then we must walk in love. Just as in every aspect of our walk with the Lord, we must rely on the Holy Spirit to keep us on the right path. We must walk in the Spirit not the flesh. Walking in the Spirit is synonymous with walking with God, and walking in Love. The three are different identifiers for the Deity we know as our God. The Holy Spirit is an extension of God, given to us when we accept Jesus who rose from the dead and death on the cross. Then Peter said to them, "Repent, and let every one of you be baptized in the name of Jesus Christ for the remission of sins; and you shall receive the gift of the Holy Spirit (Acts 2:38 NKJV).

So what are we talking about here? A love so deep we cannot understand as humans, but that we must understand as a child of God; a love that we can only walk in with the intimacy of our relationship with Jesus and with the guidance of the Holy Spirit. How do we in all our fleshly sinfulness pass this true love on to our children? We can only allow it to manifest in our lives through the fruit of the Spirit. As this love is displayed in our lives others will see it and this glorifies God who we are obeying. Remember all things are possible through Christ Jesus. Sometimes we only apply that to obstacles that we encounter here in this world. We should claim that in all aspects of our spiritual lives. For the most unloving person, God's true love is possible; we have a responsibility to partner with the Spirit to bring about this manifestation.

> The world's definition of love pales in comparison to the love of God.

> But also for this very reason, giving all diligence, add to your faith virtue, to virtue knowledge, to knowledge self-control, to self-control perseverance, to perseverance godliness, to godliness brotherly kindness, and to brotherly kindness love. For if these things are yours and abound, you will be neither barren nor unfruitful in the knowledge of our Lord Jesus Christ. For he who lacks these things is shortsighted, even to blindness, and has forgotten that he was cleansed from his old sins. (2 Peter 1:5-9 NKJV)

Our partnering responsibility with the Holy Spirit is to exercise diligence adding on to the faith we first professed, to reach this godly state of love. In the bible, in the second book called Peter we are taught to diligently add these characteristics, so that we will never be barren or unfruitful in the knowledge of Jesus Christ. This list of characteristics that we are responsible to take on to receive a more divine or godly nature, starts with faith and ends with God's love (defined in the KJV as charity). So our roadmap starts with faith and ends with the manifestation of God's love, real love.

Identity Principle

God's love is a love that we can only consistently show through intimacy in our relationship with Jesus & the guidance of the Holy Spirit.

Perfect Love

> There is no fear in love; but perfect love casts out fear, because fear involves torment. But he who fears has not been made perfect in love. (1 John 4:18 NKJV)

God is love; I think we have all got that. The reality of love is what is hard for us to fathom living in this world. Love in the world is more focused on lust and personal desire. The world's love is mostly selfish, and God's love example is His son Jesus Christ crucified on a cross.

What about fear? See, God did not give us a spirit of fear, but of power, love and a sound mind (2 Tim.1:7). We have to walk in the contentment that God loves us and will not harm us. Whatever we go through in Christ is for our ultimate good and the purposes of God and His glory. What we are afraid of cannot and will not ultimately kill us, if we believe that God will never leave us or forsake us. As a child of God no weapon formed against us shall prosper. This means that no attack of the enemy or tragedy in this world can take our life or ultimately destroy us if we trust and believe in God. Remember our life as children of God is in Christ Jesus. Physical death just means the beginning of eternal life in heaven with God. Do you have the faith to believe that?

Identity Principle

No attack of the enemy or tragedy in this world can take our life or ultimately destroy us if we trust & believe in God.

The scripture says that perfect love casts out fear. We are to be made perfect in love, perfected in the love of God. Our fear is cast out because God so loved the world that He gave His only begotten Son, that whosoever believes in Him shall not perish, but have everlasting life. He loved us before we came to Him with all our sin, how much more does He love us now as His children.

> The end of all things is near. Therefore be clear minded and self-controlled so that you can pray. Above all, love each other deeply, because love covers over a multitude of sins (1 Peter 4:7-8 NRSV)

At this point in the reading we should be clear on the fact that we are supposed to love. Does this mean that you have love perfected, and apply love in every situation in your life; probably not. Usually when we don't apply love, we are caught up in an emotional state and are reacting instead of moving in a controlled (self-control) action. We have all been in a situation where we are tired and someone innocently walks into the line of fire with a comment that sets our tongue off, spouting ugly words that don't show love. Or we are so caught up in how tired we are that we don't see when someone else really needs us, so we brush them off instead of taking the opportunity to show the love of Christ. Does the

Lord ever brush you off when you need Him? Does the Lord ever not show you the love you desire? Even if you feel that God has not showed you love, I have faith and trust that God will eventually show Himself to you, in His perfect timing, the love that you really need. If you are consistent in your day to day spiritual walk, and renew your mind, then you will see that all the love God needs to show you was already done when Jesus Christ. God's only Son died on the cross for us. That is enough love for every moment of our lives.

> Love covers a multitude of sins.

In the book of first Peter, verse 7 gives us guidance so that we will not stray from showing the love that God desires us to walk in. Peter tells us first, to be clear minded. Think back to the last time you gave a sordid emotional response. Were you clear minded, or were you caught up in your feelings, not able to listen to the prompting of the Holy Spirit? Having a clear mind allows us to receive from God on the action we should take to be in line with His will for our lives. This clarity comes when we practice hearing His voice over ours and Satan. Second, we must practice self-control. All throughout God's Word we are taught to be self-controlled. This fruit of the Spirit enables us to obey what the Lord desires us to do after we hear His guidance. Then enters the need to pray for strength to carry out what the Lord would have you to do. Doing the right thing is not always easy!

Servants and followers of God, we can only walk in love as we walk in the Spirit. Walking in the Spirit and not in the flesh is only possible when we are one with God through the indwelling guidance of the Holy Spirit. Did you read verse 8? The word cover can be defined as, to compensate or make up for; or to be sufficient to defray, meet, or offset the cost or charge of (sin). All of the sin we commit each day that is forgiven on the cross of Christ, can also be covered as we show love, God's love to one another.

But the fruit of the Spirit is love, joy, peace, longsuffering, kindness, goodness, faithfulness, gentleness, self-control. Against such there is no law. And those who are Christ's have crucified the flesh with its passions and desires. If we live in the Spirit, let us also walk in the Spirit. Let us not become conceited, provoking one another, envying one another (Galatians 5:22-26 NKJV).

The Grey Area

Truly understanding the breadth and depth of God's love for us is the adhesive that will hold our faith together. If we can only continuously keep our eyes on the cross of Christ, and identify with the love of God that allowed His only begotten Son to die that brutal and ugly death for us; then we will never move out of the place of remembering His love. Once we have embraced the love for ourselves, we will not be able to help ourselves; we will have to tell the world and our children about the love that is waiting for us, beckoning to us and calling us to a better way of living. This is our responsibility, our mandate, and our desire if we have the presence of the Holy Spirit in our lives.

> We can snatch back the definition of love from the world.

The Word tells us that love covers a multitude of sins. Love prevails throughout scripture and dominates every aspect of the new nature that is being perfected inside us by the work of the Holy Spirit. So where is the grey area in love? Love is supposed to conquer all. Well, the grey area is waiting to confine us and our children as the world distorts love and declares its definition as true. How are you teaching your children love? How are you displaying love to those around you? If you are not operating in the Spirit of love, then you might be fostering confusion, and God is not the author of confusion (1 Corinth. 14:33). This grey area between the worlds love and God's love can destroy families, friendships, and lead our children into the arms of death. We must show love in a godly manner consistently and openly. This will combat the false sense of love that the world shows our children in sex and in material things. We must show love in how we speak to each other, embrace one another, respect one another, and forgive one another. Seek the Lord on your walk of love, and God will be faithful to show you His way, and we can snatch back the definition of love from the world.

AGREEMENT

DECLARATION: Repeat these out loud...*and then answer the question.*

1. ***I agree that my personal relationship with God is the foundation for truth, understanding and everlasting love.*** Do you have a personal relationship with the Lord?

2. ***I agree that God will empower me to love as we are commanded to love!***
   Name one way you recognize God empowering you to love in your life.

3. ***I agree that it is my responsibility to partner with the Holy Spirit to diligently grow my faith to godly love!***

4. ***I agree that God's perfect love casts out any fear in my heart as I trust Him to help me be clear-minded and self-controlled.***

Action for Abundant Life

AWARENESS: Do you believe that God can help you apply love in all your relationships? How do you seek Him to help you love better?

AWARENESS: Have you showed love in a godly manner consistently and openly? Can you name one example?

UNDERSTANDING: Which Identity Principle in this chapter did you relate to the most? Why?

Life & Love

Seek perfection when it comes to love.
Seek the One who sits high above.
He will send His love down,
To fill your every need.
Jesus the Christ, with His love you will be freed.

True Love only comes from heaven above.
Real love,
Agape love,
The 1 Corinthians 13 kind,
Will envelop your soul, heart and mind.

This love I feel is oh so real,
It fills me up so that my heart erupts.
Call His name, for His love He freely gives.
Accept Jesus in your heart and in Him you can live.

WLS

4
AN AUTHENTIC RELATIONSHIP

John 4^{23} *But the hour is coming, and now is, when the true worshipers will worship the Father in spirit and truth; for the Father is seeking such to worship Him. (NKJV)*

WILL GOD THE FATHER FIND YOU as He seeks those who worship Him in spirit and in truth? The only way we can answer this question is if we know what Spirit we are worshipping. If you are a child of God, then there is only one Spirit that your internal spirit bears witness of.

> The Spirit Himself bears witness with our spirit that we are children of God. (Romans 8:16 NKJV)

> This is He who came by water and blood—Jesus Christ; not only by water, but by water and blood. And it is the Spirit who bears witness, because the Spirit is truth. (1 John 5:6 NKJV)

We were given the Holy Spirit when we accepted Jesus Christ as our Lord and Savior. The Holy Spirit is the only Spirit we should be filled with. The Spirit indwells us and empowers us to do all things through Christ Jesus. What spirit are you walking in? What spirit are you exhibiting in your life?

Generational Spirits

We hear so much these days about being spiritual. What does being spiritual really mean? If you are spiritual, which spirit are you acknowledging? The devil is a spirit and seeks to use us for his evil purposes. When we just accept any old spirit we are open to such things as witchcraft, sorcery, and fleshly behavior.

Identity Principle

When we just accept any spirit we are open to such things as witchcraft, sorcery, and fleshy sinful behavior.

These spirits battle the Holy Spirit because they are feeding the flesh, and can battle the Lord as He tries to lead you and guide you to walk a holy and righteous life in Christ. If you are seeking the guidance of other spirits through witchcraft, astrology, or any other way we seek to find out the future, then you quench the Holy Spirit and are walking in the flesh. You are potentially not clearly hearing the voice of the Lord resident inside of you, because you are taking the guidance of the other god or spirit over the Lords'.

> And he built altars for all the host of heaven in the two courts of the house of the LORD. Also he made his son pass through the fire, practiced soothsaying, used witchcraft, and consulted spiritists and mediums. He did much evil in the sight of the LORD, to provoke Him to anger. (2 Kings 21:5-6 NKJV)

> "When you come into the land which the LORD your God is giving you, you shall not learn to follow the abominations of those nations. There shall not be found among you anyone who makes his son or his daughter pass through the fire, or one who practices witchcraft, or a soothsayer, or one who interprets omens, or a sorcerer, or one who conjures spells, or a medium, or a spiritist, or one who calls up the dead. (Deuteronomy 18:9-11 NKJV)

The Truth

We have established who the one true Spirit is, and how we have to know what spirit we are worshiping. Now we need to understand what the Father means by 'in truth'. We might say we understand what is meant by truth, but do we really. If we are going on what we have learned in school or even from someone we trust, our definition might be skewed. See the truth is not something that is logically determined or rationally derived. Understanding 'truth' can only come from God.

> Jesus said to him, "I am the way, the truth, and the life. No one comes to the Father except through Me. (John 14:6 NKJV)

> "But when the Helper comes, whom I shall send to you from the Father, the Spirit of truth who proceeds from the Father, He will testify of Me. (John 15:26 NKJV)

Unless you have received the Holy Spirit, there is no way you can know the 'truth'. The Word says in spirit and in truth; the spirit comes first because there is no way you can get to truth without the Spirit. Jesus imparts truth through His gift of the Holy Spirit. So we have the Holy Spirit in us, from Jesus, speaking to us from God. We have the power of the Godhead, all working for and with us as God the Father, God the Son, and God the Holy Spirit imparting truth.

> And you shall know the truth, and the truth shall make you free."(John 8:32 NKJV)

Identity Principle

The Word says in spirit and in truth; the spirit comes first because there is no way you can see the truth without the Holy Spirit.

Truth frees us up from the trappings of the world and the lies of the enemy. Truth brings us to an understanding of who we are and what our purpose is in the family of God. We have a direct connection through our personal relationship with Christ, to understand the truth and what it means for us. It is one thing to know the truth, and it is another to walk in it. What do you mean walk in it? Well, we have been discussing what it means to be a child of God and the importance of passing on the faith. We also explored how those coming behind us and others we see every day pay more attention to what we do than what we say. What we do every day, how we respond to situations, and what we speak out of our mouths testifies to the Jesus in us. We are the only Jesus some people will ever see. So when we walk in the truth, we are walking in the manner that the Lord walked when He was on earth. We are walking in communion and in constant conversation with the Holy Spirit. We are walking in God's will for our lives, living life the way the Word of God prescribes.

> And the Word became flesh and dwelt among us, and we beheld His glory, the glory as of the only begotten of the Father, full of grace and truth. (John 1:14)
>
> For the law was given through Moses, but grace and truth came through Jesus Christ. (John 1:17)

We have to understand God's written truth, but there is also the revealed truth that the Spirit ministers to us as we read the Word or as we are listening to the proclaimed or preached Word of God. The Word is living and active, it is applicable to every situation you will ever be in. There is what we see and hear, and then there is the truth as revealed by God through His Holy Spirit. The Lord will lead you and guide you in and through every situation. We cannot lean on our own understanding of life, or else there is the possibility we can be highly disillusioned, and potentially depressed. God's ways are higher than our ways and His thoughts are higher than our thoughts.

Identity Principle

> What we do every day, how we respond to situations, and what we speak out of our mouths testifies to the Jesus in us.

We cannot figure out God, that is why He gave us His Holy Spirit to reveal the truth to us. Life is full of troubles and pain, and we cannot rely on our own logic to lead the way. There is a way that seems right to us, but the end of that way can lead to destruction. That is why Jesus came that we might have life, and have it more abundantly. So we cannot just stop at life, we have to seek truth; we have to take that truth and allow the Spirit to lead us to understanding so we can walk in it. The Word says in all you are getting, get understanding. When we understand what God has for us and what our purpose is, we can walk in the abundance of life Jesus has promised. Understanding can purify your soul, and by obeying the truth of God you can live with a pure heart.

> Since you have purified your souls in obeying the truth through the Spirit in sincere love of the brethren, love one another fervently with a pure heart, having been born again, not of corruptible seed but incorruptible, through the word of God which lives and abides forever. (1 Peter 1:22-23 NKJV)

The Father of Lies

Let's call him what he is, a liar. Satan is a deceiver, that comes but to steal, kill and destroy our lives (John 10:10). We have the truth if we are a child of God. We have the secret weapon, the antidote; we have the armor of the Holy Spirit and the Word of God. If we look at life from the world's perspective we see death, despair, and we can feel defeated. That is how Satan wants it. Life as a child of God is not simply a humdrum, mundane task that we are immersed in with no hope. We have been redeemed from this world, and we are not subject to the tricks of the enemy.

> Let's call Satan what he is, a liar!

We have the Word of God to combat him and to know his tricks. We can stand up to his attacks and know that God is ultimately in control, and that no weapon formed against us shall prosper. Whatever the enemy thinks he is defeating us with, will not get the results he desires. We will not die, we will not be defeated. What Satan means for evil, God is faithful to turn around for our good, no matter how it feels when we are going through the situation. We have hope where there is no hope, and we have a Savior whose burden is easy and whose yoke is light. We see the enemy for who he is and must understand why those who don't know the Lord, act, say and behave as they do. So let's review what God says about those in the world.

> The Spirit of truth, whom the world cannot receive, because it neither sees Him nor knows Him; but you know Him, for He dwells with you and will be in you. (John 14:17 NKJV)

> You are of your father the devil, and the desires of your father you want to do. He was a murderer from the beginning, and does not stand in the truth, because there is no truth in him. When he speaks a lie, he speaks from his own resources, for he is a liar and the father of it. (John 8:44 NKJV)

We are blessed to know the Lord. In Him we have hope, without Him there is no hope, just death. We are to seek the Lord by reading and understanding who He is and His character in His Word, so we as one body in Christ can know the truth and walk in it in unity. The Holy Spirit is faithful to bring us individually to all understanding, so that we can be the church that the Lord is coming back for without blemish or without spot.

> And if you call on the Father, who without partiality judges according to each one's work, conduct yourselves throughout the time of your stay here in fear; knowing that you were not redeemed with corruptible things, like silver or gold, from your aimless conduct received by tradition from your fathers, but with the precious blood of Christ, as of a lamb without blemish and without spot. He indeed was foreordained before the foundation of the world, but was manifest in these last times for you who through Him believe in God, who raised Him from the dead and gave Him glory, so that your faith and hope are in God. (1 Peter 1:17-21 NKJV)

Alcohol As A Deterrent

> Woe to the proud crown of the drunkards of E'phraim, and to the fading flower of its glorious beauty, which is

on the head of the rich valley of those overcome with wine! Behold, the Lord has one who is mighty and strong; like a storm of hail, a destroying tempest, like a storm of mighty, overflowing waters, he will cast down to the earth with violence. The proud crown of the drunkards of E'phraim will be trodden under foot; and the fading flower of its glorious beauty, which is on the head of the rich valley, will be like a first-ripe fig before the summer: when a man sees it, he eats it up as soon as it is in his hand.
These also reel with wine and stagger with strong drink; the priest and the prophet reel with strong drink, they are confused with wine, they stagger with strong drink; they err in vision, they stumble in giving judgment. For all tables are full of vomit, no place is without filthiness. (Isaiah 28:1-4;7-8)

Alcohol is meant to be intoxicating. Intoxication as defined by the American Heritage Dictionary means, stupefaction or excitement by the action of a chemical substance, or Webster defines it as a high excitement, frenzy or madness"; Alcohol is defined as a pure spirit of wine; pure or highly rectified spirit (called also ethyl alcohol); the spirituous or intoxicating element of fermented or distilled liquors, or more loosely a liquid containing it in considerable quantity.

Identity Principle

When we are intoxicated with anything else but the Holy Spirit, we can be blocked from hearing God clearly. This can cause us to stray out of God's will.

The Lord wants us to be full of His Spirit. When we indulge the flesh with an alternate intoxication, such as alcohol, we are filled with that drug and therefore cannot be completely aware or full of the Holy Spirit. The Holy Spirit is 'indwelling' or in us (continuously because the Spirit lives in us) if we are a child of God, and we can be 'full or filled with the Spirit', which is a repeat experience.

Being intoxicated is also defined by Wordnet as *'a temporary state resulting from excessive consumption of alcohol'*. When we consume alcohol it is usually for the temporary effect it gives us. This action becomes an escape and then a habit. Thus we depend on it for a quick fix instead of receiving a lasting fix from God. When we are intoxicated with anything else but the Holy Spirit, we can be blocked from hearing God clearly. This can cause us to stray out of God's will.

The prophet Isaiah is attempting to speak to the people of Ephraim in Jerusalem as they have become drunkards and are worshiping false gods. We clearly see that Isaiah states that through intoxication the people are out of the way of God. They err in vision and judgment as they cannot hear or follow God's Word. There are several examples in the bible where the people are 'drunk' and are in a position where they are not in the state of mind to hear the message God has for them. (See Proverbs 23:29-35 and Ephesians 5:14-20) The point is not that you are drinking, but that you drink to get drunk. The Word of God says that He will be your comforter and will not leave you comfortless by sending you his Holy Spirit (John 14:16). When you get drunk you can feel freer to say whatever comes to your mind, or do whatever your flesh feels. The devil is very smart. He thinks if I can get them drunk, then it will be even harder for them to resist temptation and obey God. Once we make a move away from God toward following our flesh, the devil just comes at us from every direction, using our flesh to push us further from righteousness. I say then: Walk in the Spirit, and you shall not fulfill the lust of the flesh (Galatians 5:16). God gives us guidance for our lives, and we need to be able to hear Him clearly so that we can be the servant He desires loving one another.

> Alcohol is usually used for its temporary effect; it becomes an escape and then a habit.

Identity Principle

The devil is very smart. He thinks if I can get them drunk, then it will be even harder for them to resist temptation and obey God.

The Grey Area

The resurrecting power of Jesus Christ has allowed us to walk and worship in Spirit and in truth. Are we doing it? Are we setting the right example for the youth of today? Can your children, your nieces and nephews, or the children you come in contact with on a daily bases see or sense that there is a spirit about you that is different from what they would normally see in the world? If not, what spirit are you showing them? Team spirit as you root for your favorite football team. Or do they see the power of the spirit of astrology as you proclaim to them how your horoscope was exactly on point today. Are you testifying of the way the Holy Spirit warned you not to take the interstate today, and that you later found out about an accident? What spirit are you glorifying? What has potentially stolen your worship?

> The Lord wants us to be full of His Spirit.

This is the grey area we place our children in when we don't walk in truth. This grey area leads them away from the truth of the Word to the truth of the world. Our behavior confuses them, and we know that God is not the author of confusion (1 Corinth. 14:33). What do they believe when someone tells them to go with them to have their palm read, and they start looking to the palm reader for guidance and direction instead of the Holy Spirit? How have we set an example for them, if we believe God on Sunday and Wednesday, but every other day we need to read the horoscope to know what to expect? God is faithful to tell us what we need to know beforehand (John 14:25-29). His Word says that He will make our crooked places straight and reveal to us His great mysteries. If God planned our whole life before we were even in our mother's womb, then why would we look to anyone or anything else for understanding or guidance? Everything we do has consequences. Every step we take should be made with prayerful contemplation, and we should be mindful of the example we are setting. Let's not leave the choices of our children to chance. Let's show them the one true Spirit, and allow them to see us walking in truth so their path does not take the wrong turn in the grey area.

AGREEMENT

DECLARATION: *Repeat these out loud...and then answer the question.*

1. ***I agree that the only spirit I will be "FULL OF" is the Holy Spirit!***

2. ***I agree that the Holy Spirit lives inside me and gives me the power to do ALL things through Christ Jesus!***
   Name one way you recognize God empowering you by His Spirit.

3. ***I agree that the truth is not logically determined or rationally derived BUT can only come from God.***

4. ***I agree that Satan is a liar and a deceiver. I know that I have the Word of God to combat him and to know his tricks.***

5. ***I agree that I can and will walk in the Spirit and will not fulfill the lust of the flesh!***

Action for Abundant Life

AWARENESS: Do people you come in contact with see a different spirit than the one that is normally seen in the world?
Can you give an example?

UNDERSTANDING: Which Identity Principle in this chapter did you relate to the most? Why?

Wanda L. Scott

Whose spirit do you display?
What truth do you follow today?
Whose child are you?
Whose guidance will get you through?

Examine your ways so you can see.
Test your faithfulness,
the Holy Spirit will allow you to see – the truth.

God is faithful,
an authentic relationship with Him you can obtain.
Just trust and believe that
in His Word you will receive,
Peace
Joy
Love
With Him you will be free indeed.

WLS

5
GOD'S FAMILY PORTRAIT

1 Corinthians 12 [12] *For just as the body is one and has many members, and all the members of the body, though many, are one body, so it is with Christ.* [13] *For by one Spirit we were all baptized into one body—Jews or Greeks, slaves or free—and all were made to drink of one Spirit.* [14] *For the body does not consist of one member but of many. (NKJV)*

CONCEPTUALLY THE STATEMENT THAT WE ARE the body of Christ is somewhat hard to grasp. It is easier to understand that we are a child of God, and the difference between the lust/love of the world versus the 'agape love' of God. If we are diligently studying the Word of God, and are walking in the Spirit and in Love, which are one in the same, then we are treating others with the love that we would want to receive in return. This makes the path to 'one body in Christ' a little easier to walk. If we are already treating others as we would want to be treated, then we are treating them as we would treat ourselves. So essentially they are a part of us, as we are joined and knit together by what every joint supplies, according to the effective working by which every part does its share (Ephesians 4:16). If one of the body is fallen or walking in continual sin (iniquity), then they could not be walking in the Spirit. That member of the body is failing to glorify God, and is not being obedient to the Spirit, thus the body is not functioning at full capacity. The body is sick. That member of the body is not walking in the abundant life promised by Jesus if we are obedient. Satan has come in, and has been allowed to steal, kill and destroy their faith. We see in Paul's letter to the Galatians that we are to bear each other's burdens in a spirit of gentleness, restoring each other if we are spiritual.

Brethren, if a man is overtaken in any trespass, you who are spiritual restore such a one in a spirit of gentleness, considering yourself lest you also be tempted. Bear one another's burdens, and so fulfill the law of Christ (Galatians 6:1-2).

Becoming a part of the body of Christ does not just conceptually change how we think of ourselves and one another; it by definition changes our every decision and action. If we are the body, with Jesus Christ as our head, then we don't make our own decisions anymore. Jesus is Lord of our life. Lord is defined as someone or something that is in authority over you. So Christ as our head, as our Lord, has authority over our lives and determines each and every move we make. Biologically every part of the body has a response determined by the impulse from the mind or 'head'. Psychologically, our responses to life and others should be different also, because we have a different standard, as defined by the Word of God. Jesus is our Head, therefore we have God as our Head giving us godly responses that line us with the fruit of the Spirit (Galatians 5:22). We don't respond the world's way according to our flesh, with hate, anger, or lust. We respond according to what we study and meditate on, which should be the Word of God. We function with our mind and eyes on Jesus, our Lord and Savior.

Identity Principle

Being part of the body of Christ changes our every decision and action. If we are the body, then we don't make our own decisions anymore.

Life & Love

The ideal function of the body of Christ is to move in harmony, displaying the fruit of the Spirit – love, joy, peace, self-control, patience, kindness, gentleness, and brotherly love. In order to bear the fruit, we have to be in the Spirit. Think about how hard it can be to just get along with family that you live with every day; whether they are children of God or not. Dysfunction in our homes can transfer outside of the home to other relational environments. This dysfunction is typically learned behavior that has to be transformed by the renewing of our minds (Romans 12:1-2). Depending on when you accepted Jesus and became spiritually the body of Christ, and how intentional you and others were about your maturation and growth, there is a strong possibility that you have been conformed to this world and its ways. This learned behavior can be a dangerous mix of worldliness with a "form of godliness". The Word clearly declares that we cannot serve two masters. This poses an extra effort on our part, in conjunction with the Holy Spirit to transform those "old" ways to the new and perfected thinking aligned with our head (Jesus). This transformation can only take place as the Word of God is read, studied, and applied to our everyday lives. Then the Holy Spirit will be able to outwardly manifest the fruit of the Spirit that is in us.

> But as for you, speak the things which are proper for sound doctrine: that the older men be sober, reverent, temperate, sound in faith, in love, in patience; the older women likewise, that they be reverent in behavior, not slanderers, not given to much wine, teachers of good things— that they admonish the young women to love their husbands, to love their children, to be discreet, chaste, homemakers, good, obedient to their own husbands, that the word of God may not be blasphemed. Likewise, exhort the young men to be sober-minded, in all things showing yourself to be a pattern of good works; in doctrine showing integrity, reverence, incorruptibility, sound speech that cannot be condemned, that one who is an opponent may be ashamed, having nothing evil to say of you.
> (Titus 2:1-8)

Identity Principle

We should be striving to walk in Harmony and as a good example to one another, teaching and cautioning one another to do what is right in God's eyes.

Not only is harmony something we should be striving for, but the ability to walk as a good example to one another, teaching and admonishing one another to do what is right in God's eyes. This is what we see in the apostle Paul's letter to Titus, as he instructs him on what he should teach, and how the body of Christ should act toward one another. There are several characteristics that are outlined for older men and women, and younger men and women. So at every age in the body of Christ we are recognized and responsible to each other. If we make an effort to walk out these characteristics, then we will be a good example as well as in position to be in harmony as one body in Christ.

The Body of Christ as a Family

We have become familiar with the body and the need for it to function as one body in Christ in harmony. Now we, moving in harmony, should love one another as a family.

> The individual members of God's body are not always walking in the Spirit that God has placed in them.

This family we are grafted into introduces us to new brothers and sisters in Christ. We also inherit mothers and fathers in the Spirit who act as leaders and sources of wisdom as we walk with the Lord. These new relations serve in several capacities, so that we can strengthen each other as we fellowship and serve the Lord together. The Word calls for us to encourage each other, edify one another, restore, and admonish the body, as well as to hold each other accountable in our daily living.

These tasks are not to be taken lightly, and selections of who we allow to carry them out in our lives should be approached with much prayer and discernment. Although we are one body, we are not all always walking in the Spirit that God has placed in us. We must sincerely seek the Lord on every relationship we participate in, including the familial relationships that we inherit.

Identity Principle

We must sincerely seek the Lord on every relationship we participate in, including the familial relationships that we inherit in Christ.

So we see that not only are we one body, utterly dependent on one another, but we also are a family of believers adopted by the Spirit of God to dwell in harmony with one another. The early Christian church laid a foundation that has allowed for us to call people of all nations, races and cultures our family, spiritually tied together by one awesome God.

Family Regardless of Culture

Just as when Jesus walked this earth, He did not restrict His ministry to one culture or another; we must not do that today. Our worship and fellowship must be led by the Spirit, not by preferences or convenience. The Lord is no respecter of persons. Love does not regard color, love does not judge, but looks for the good. So we must deal with differences with Love. We must be open to conversation about how we can meet the needs of all people without compromising the gospel of Jesus Christ. In all things we remember that if we are serving the true and living God, we will be able to function in the Spirit and worship Him in Spirit and in truth regardless of what color or culture is represented when we are in fellowship with one another. When we are able to clearly understand in our minds the encapsulation of one body, one mind, one Spirit, then we can live out the scriptural definition of the body of Christ. Then we will walk as one body, glorifying God. When we get to this state of being, and the body is functioning as one, drinking of one Spirit, we will know we are in the midst of the real body of Christ; the church of the living God.

The Grey Area

As in every aspect of retaining our identity in Christ we meet the grey area when trying to truly live out the familial aspect of the body of Christ. There are so many obstacles in the flesh to maintaining the unity that Christ desires. It is at this crossroads where we are finally trying to find our place in the body, and we meet up with opposition from those who are supposed to be that 'one body in Christ'. Here we can become jaded and decide that these people are no better than the ones in the world. Here we have to make a decision for Christ and not for mankind. Here we have to stand on our faith, and not waver in what we have started building our foundation on; which should be Jesus Christ. Even though we are spiritual and new creatures in Christ, we still have this treasure in earthen vessels. We still have to die to the flesh daily in order to walk in the Spirit of Christ. So there is going to be occasion for the flesh to take over, and disobedience to have its way in a child of God' life. Once disobedience rears its ugly head, the enemy has room to try and cause us to doubt, and to try and destroy our move toward abundant life in Jesus. We must not get lost there, we must press on toward Jesus believing that God has conquered the enemy, the devil, and whatever spirit that is rearing its ugly head up against us.

If we have spent any time in a local church or in fellowship with other believers we know the tricks and traps of the enemy. The enemy never leaves himself unrepresented, even in our fellowship. As we press through the grey area, there is a need to be fully armored with the Word in order to prevail. If we have made it to this point and are trying to consistently be pleasing in

God's sight, then we are really on the enemies "hit list". Be encouraged and put on the full armor of God.

> Finally, my brethren, be strong in the Lord and in the power of His might. Put on the whole armor of God, that you may be able to stand against the wiles of the devil. For we do not wrestle against flesh and blood, but against principalities, against powers, against the rulers of the darkness of this age, against spiritual hosts of wickedness in the heavenly places. Therefore take up the whole armor of God, that you may be able to withstand in the evil day, and having done all, to stand. Stand therefore, having girded your waist with truth, having put on the breastplate of righteousness, and having shod your feet with the preparation of the gospel of peace; above all, taking the shield of faith with which you will be able to quench all the fiery darts of the wicked one. And take the helmet of salvation, and the sword of the Spirit, which is the word of God; praying always with all prayer and supplication in the Spirit, being watchful to this end with all perseverance and supplication for all the saints— (Ephesians 6:10-18 NKJV)

Identity Principle

If we are serving the true and living God, we will be able to worship Him in Spirit and in truth regardless of what color or culture is represented when we are in fellowship with one another.

AGREEMENT

DECLARATION: Repeat these out loud...*and then answer the question.*

1. ***I agree that I am a part of the body of Christ and I don't make my own decisions anymore.***
   Do you allow Jesus to determine your responses to your daily situations?

2. ***I agree to allow the Word of God to transform my life through reading it, studying it and applying it to my everyday life!***
   Name one way you recognize God transforming your life.

3. ***I agree to strive for harmony in the body of Christ through the power of the Holy Spirit.***

4. ***I agree that I am a part of one body, utterly dependent on one another, as a family of believers adopted by the Spirit of God to dwell in harmony.***

Action for Abundant Life

AWARENESS: Do you believe that you can operate in the unity God desires?
Name one situation where you have seen God unite His people.

AWARENESS: Have you put on the full amour of God instead of reacting in your flesh to a bad situation amongst the body of believers? Give one example?

UNDERSTANDING: Which Identity Principle in this chapter did you relate to the most?   Why?

One body in Christ,
a family by faith
Tied to each other,
as spiritual lovers.

One Leader we follow,
Jesus is His name.
He is the head of lives,
His ways we proclaim.

We are to walk with
…one faith
…one spirit
…one mind
Our intentions the same.

Help us dear Lord
as your children.
So your love we will not be
put to shame.

WLS

Notes

Notes

Notes

Notes

Bibliography

WHO ARE YOU?
1. Alan Jones, *Exploring Spiritual Direction* (Boston: Cowley Publications, 1999), p.9
2. Charles Stanley, *Success God's Way* (Nashville: Thomas Nelson, 2000), p. 11
3. Stanley, p. 12
4. Stanley, p. 12
5. Stanley, p. 13
6. Stanley, p. 17

YOU: DESIGNED BY GOD
1. Dr. Myles Monroe, *Understanding the Purpose and Power of Men* (New Kingston: Whitaker House, 2001), p. 27

Scripture References

WHO ARE YOU?
Philippians 2:14 – 16 (NRSV), p. 7 Romans 6:15-23 (KJV), p. 8 Deuteronomy 11:18-21 (KJV), p. 12 1 John 2:15-17 (NKJV), p. 15 Revelation 12:9-12 (NKJV), p. 16 John 10:10, p. 16 Ephesians 2:1-3 (NKJV), p. 16 1 Peter 2:9 (NKJV), p. 17

YOU: DESIGNED BY GOD
Genesis 1:27-28 (NRSV), p. 21 1 John 5:1 (NRSV), p. 21 John 1:12 (NRSV), p. 21 1 John 3:1 (NRSV), p. 21 2 Corinthians 4:6, p. 27 Romans 8:16 (NKJV), p. 22 Romans 9:8 (NKJV), p. 22 2 Corinthians 5:17, p. 23 1 John 3:10 (NKJV), p. 23 1 John 5:2 (NRSV), p. 23 Galatians 2:20 (NKJV), p. 24 Revelation 3:20, p. 24 1 Corinthians 12:7 (NKJV), p. 24 2 Corinthians 13:5-6 (NKJV), p. 24 John 16:33, p. 25 Hebrews 7:25 (NKJV), p. 25 Ephesians 2:8-10 (NKJV), p. 26 Colossians 3:3 (NKJV), p. 26 Luke 18:18, p.26

WHAT IS REAL LOVE
1 Corinthians 13:7 (NRSV), p. 31 2 Corinthians 4:6 (NKJV), p. 31 1 Corinthians 13:4-8 (NKJV), p. 32 Acts 2:38, p. 33 2 Peter 1:5-9 (NKJV), p. 33 1 John 4:18 (NKJV), p. 34 2 Timothy 1:7, p. 34 1 Peter 4:7-8 (NRSV), p. 35 Galatians 5:22-26 (NKJV), p. 37 1 Corinthians 14:33, p. 38

AN AUTHENTIC RELATIONSHIP
John 4:23 (NKJV), p. 42 Romans 8:16 (NKJV), p. 42 1 John 5:6 (NKJV), p. 42 2 Kings 21:5-6 (NKJV), p. 43 Deuteronomy 18:9-11 (NKJV), p. 43 John 14:16, p. 44 John 15:26 (NKJV), p. 44 John 8:32 (NKJV), p. 44 John 1:14 (NKJV), p. 45 John 1:17 (NKJV), p. 45 1 Peter 1:22-23 (NKJV), p. 46 John 14:17 (NKJV), p. 47 John 8:44 (NKJV), p. 47 1 Peter 1:17-21 (NKJV), p. 47 Isaiah 28:1-4;7-8 (NKJV), p. 48 John 14:25-29, p. 50

GOD'S FAMILY PORTRAIT
1 Corinthians 12:12-14 (NKJV), p. 55 Galatians 6:1-2, p. 56 Galatians 5:22, p. 56 Romans 12:1-2, p. 57 Titus 2:1-8 (KJV), p. 57 Ephesians 6:10-18 (NKJV), p. 61

Are you ready to be Encouraged, Empowered and Educated?

Wanda L. Scott is a Speaker, Educator, Author and Consultant who *Encourages Faith, Empowers Relationships*, and *Educates others for Abundant Life*!

Rev. Wanda L. Scott has been captivating audiences for over 10 years. Invite Rev. Wanda to come deliver a powerful Word that *teaches the Power of a personal relationship with Jesus Christ, how to prioritizing Love in every Relationship, as she expounds on the Word of God educating you on "Agreement" for life in the Kingdom of God!*

Visit www.WandaLScott.com to Book Wanda and to view & purchase ALL of her ministry resources.

Connect with us:

 @WandasWalk

 Facebook.com/AuthorWandaLScott

Contact us on how we can empower your congregation!

"Moving the body of Christ from the PEWs to workers in the Kingdom of God"

Wanda L. Scott

Image Institute
Education. Consultation.

Developing A Greater You!

Wanda L. Scott is the Speaker for you on topics such as:
- *Leadership*
- *Effective Communications*
- *Women in IT*

Wanda L. Scott also offers Coaching on topics such as:
- *Leadership*
- *Taking Your Ideas from your Thoughts to Paper to Publish*
- *Preparing Authors to Speak on Tour*
- *Healthy Relationships*
- *Successfully Single*
- *Guarding the Gift*

…..**other coaching packages are available for Spiritual and Practical areas.**

www.Image-Institute.com

For Live Teachings on Periscope follow:

 **Image_Institute**

OTHER BOOKS BY WANDA L. SCOTT

Where are you in life's relationships?

What have you been through in your lifetime?

"A good poet is hard to find and welcome when she finds us. Let us welcome Wanda Scott to the family of poets." Nikki Giovanni

A Lifetime of Relationships: Letters, Poems and Words of Love is an evolution and exploration into the life of Wanda L. Scott, a journey through the tumultuous emotions of life's experiences. It is a compilation of passionate poetry reflecting on life and love, pain and powerlessness, highs and lows. This book touches you where you are in life's relationships. It will help others to reflect on their life and inquire how they can express themselves to release life's emotions.

Life has a unique way of entangling us in the midst of our relationships and emotions. Are you ready to move through life releasing instead of storing up the pain? How do you express yourself in these emotional times? How do you move past the emotional pain to spiritual healing, true love, and peace? One way is to express ourselves with letters, poems and words of love.

A Lifetime of Relationships is a vehicle to demonstrate God's power of creative expression through his children, and has a **companion workshop** that stresses *God's Word on Godly Relationships*.

To learn more about Wanda's workshops, teachings, and other resources visit her on the Web at: www.wandalscott.com

Or write:

Wanda L. Scott
P.O. Box 120804
Nashville, TN 37212-0804

"I" Can Relate
How Not To Lose Yourself in Relationships

How Are You Doing In Relationships?

The "**SHIP**" in relationship can take you down traitorous waters that can have your life turning up-side down with every high wave, flowing in the wrong direction with every misguided emotion, and heading toward a shipwreck that your heart can't stand again.

God is a God of relationship. Join us in discussing your "I" and its place in relationships. Using the wisdom in the Word of God, we will see how the Lord can guide us in relationship.

To learn more about Wanda's workshops, teachings, and other resources visit her on the Web at: www.wandalscott.com

Or write:

Wanda L. Scott
P.O. Box 120804
Nashville, TN 37212-0804

www.ingramcontent.com/pod-product-compliance
Lightning Source LLC
Chambersburg PA
CBHW050705160426
43194CB00010B/2009